SERIES EDITOR: LEE JOHNSON

OSPREY MILITARY MEN-AT-ARMS

THE NORTH-EAST FRONTIER 1837–1901

WRITTEN BY
IAN HEATH

COLOUR PLATES BY
MICHAEL PERRY

First published in Great Britain in 1999 by Osprey Publishing,
Elms Court, Chapel Way, Botley, Oxford OX2 9LP, United Kingdom

© 1999 Osprey Publishing Ltd.

All rights reserved. Apart from any fair dealing for the purpose of private study, research, criticism or review, as permitted under the Copyright, Designs and Patents Act, 1988, no part of this publication may be reproduced, stored in a retrieval system, or transmitted in any form or by any means, electronic, electrical, chemical, mechanical, optical, photocopying, recording or otherwise, without the prior written permission of the copyright owner. Enquiries should be addressed to the Publishers.

ISBN 1 85532 762 7

Military Editor: Nikolai Bogdanovic
Design: Alan Hamp/Design for Books

Origination by Renaissance, Bournemouth
Printed through World Print Ltd., Hong Kong

99 00 01 02 03   10 9 8 7 6 5 4 3 2 1

FOR A CATALOGUE OF ALL BOOKS PUBLISHED BY OSPREY MILITARY,
AVIATION AND AUTOMOTIVE PLEASE WRITE TO:

The Marketing Manager, Osprey Publishing Ltd.,
P.O. Box 140, Wellingborough, Northants NN8 4ZA,
United Kingdom

OR VISIT OSPREY'S WEBSITE AT:
http://www.osprey-publishing.co.uk

Publishers' note

Readers may wish to study this title in conjunction with the following select list of Osprey publications:

Men-at-Arms 67 *The Indian Mutiny*
Men-at-Arms 72 *North-West Frontier 1837–1947*
Men-at-Arms 91 *Bengal Cavalry Regiments 1860–1914*
Men-at-Arms 92 *Indian Infantry Regiments 1857–1914*
Men-at-Arms 193 *The British Army on Campaign (1) 1816–1853*
Men-at-Arms 198 *The British Army on Campaign (3) 1856–1881*
Men-at-Arms 201 *The British Army on Campaign (4) 1882–1902*
Men-at-Arms 212 *Queen Victoria's Enemies (3) India*
Men-at-Arms 224 *Queen Victoria's Enemies (4) Asia, Australasia and the Americas*
Men-at-Arms 268 *British Troops in the Indian Mutiny 1857–9*
Men-at-Arms 275 *The Taiping Rebellion 1851–66*

Artist's note

Readers may care to note that the original paintings from which the colour plates in this book were prepared are available for private sale. All reproduction copyright whatsoever is retained by the Publishers. All enquiries should be addressed to:

Michael Perry
Flat 3, Pevril Drive, The Park, Nottingham NG7 1DE

The Publishers regret that they can enter into no correspondence upon this matter.

THE NORTH-EAST FRONTIER
1837–1901

Despite the fact that it was events on the North-West Frontier which perennially awed and captivated Victorian audiences, British India's North-East Frontier saw at least as much military activity, and possibly even more – albeit on a generally smaller scale. Yet it remains a largely forgotten theatre of colonial warfare. There were many reasons for this: the North-East Frontier was not a potential gateway by which Russia might gain access to India; it lacked a vigorous native power comparable to Afghanistan; and by Victorian standards the Pathan tribesmen of the North-West Frontier were considered a more noble foe than their head-hunting, slave-raiding counterparts in the north-east. Nor did it help that events on the North-East Frontier were less comprehensively and less accurately covered in the press: some newspapers demonstrated appalling ignorance of the region, reporting that the campaign against the Angami Nagas in 1879–80 formed part of the Second Afghan War! Even the heroic 11-day defence of the isolated outpost of Kohima against overwhelming odds – fewer than 200 British-officered troops against perhaps 6,000 Nagas – failed to capture the public imagination. Today, after the passage of another century, Britain's numerous campaigns and conquests in Assam and the surrounding hills have faded even further into the mists of obscurity.

This lack of public awareness did not, however, diminish the potential importance of the North-East Frontier. As early as 1836 an officer observed: 'In a commercial, a statistical, or a political point of view, no country is more important. There our territory of Assam is situated in almost immediate contact with the empires of China and Ava [Burma], being separated from each by [only] a narrow belt of mountainous country'. Despite suffering defeat and substantial loss of territory in its war with the British in 1824–6, Burma, in particular, posed a significant threat to the region's security up to 1885 and was suspected of sponsoring numerous raids into British territory by frontier tribes.

Though Assam had been handed over to the British in 1765, it was left in the hands of its native ruling dynasty (the Ahoms) until 1838, by which time its commercial potential had become apparent. Optimistic entrepreneurs looked upon the jungles and foothills as an inexhaustible and lucrative source of timber, rubber and ivory. Coal and petroleum were also discovered, and vast regions of jungle were cleared for the cultivation of tea. There was only one problem: much of the best

The Garos were the first Assamese hill-people with whom the British came into contact. This remarkably accurate depiction of 'a Garrow man in his war dress' is from the report of an expedition carried out in 1788–9.

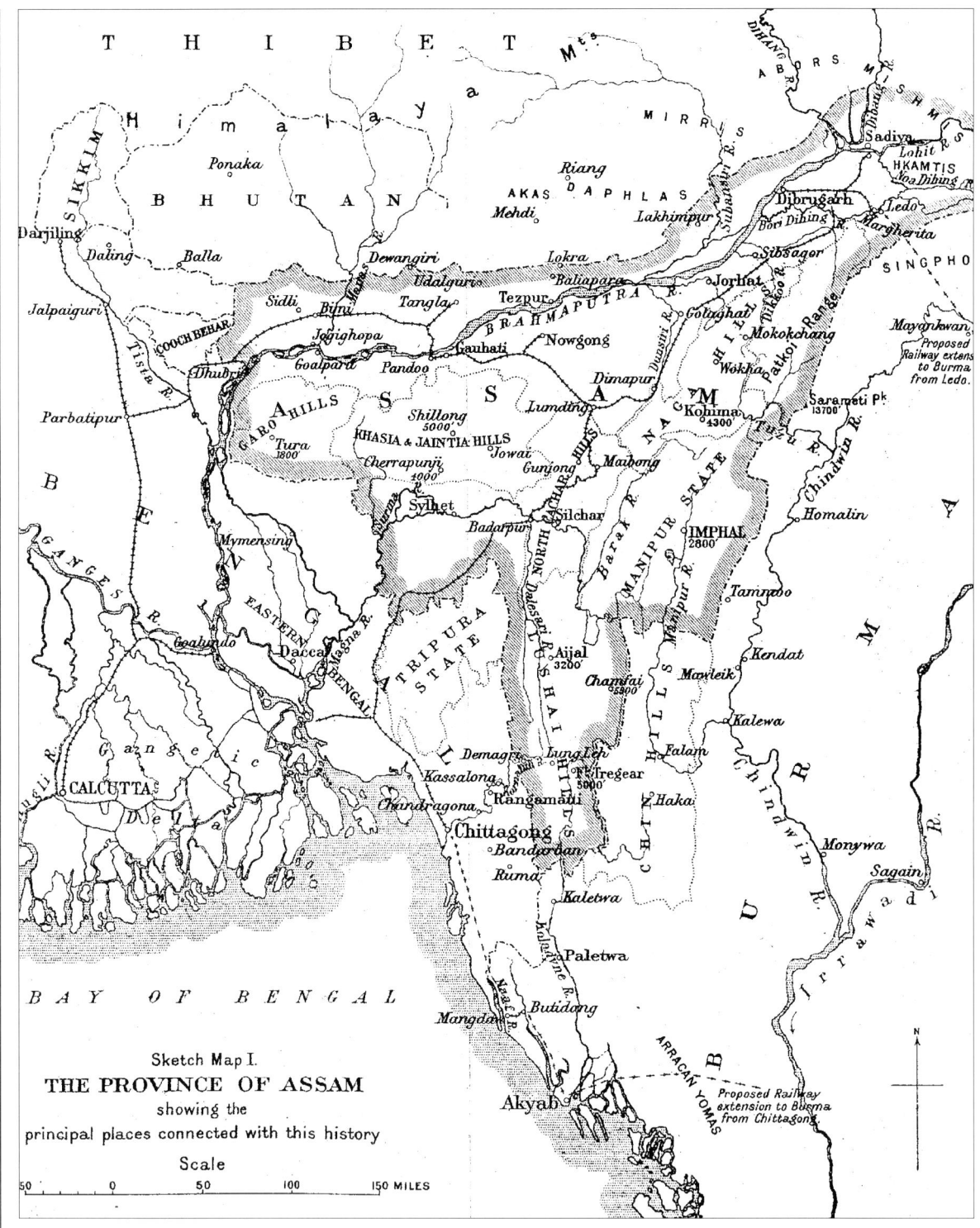

Map of Assam during the late 19th century. (L.W. Shakespear, *History of the Assam Rifles*, 1929)

land for these commercial activities was in the hands of (or threatened by) tribes with no allegiance to the British, only a passing interest in agriculture, and whose economy was based largely on slave-raiding. British attempts to suppress slaving activities meant that most of these tribes were either already hostile to the British or became so as soon as tea gardens, rubber plantations and game hunters encroached on their territory. Under such circumstances clashes were not only inevitable but commonplace.

CHRONOLOGY

Tribal feuds, murders and minor raids, as well as attacks on army and Frontier Police outposts, were almost continuous throughout the Victorian period, and on the whole the events listed here represent only the more ambitious or sanguine incidents.

1838　British remove Raja Purandar Singh (1833–8) from the throne of Upper Assam and annex all remaining independent Assamese territory. In December the British launch the second of ten expeditions mounted against the Nagas between 1835 and 1851.
1839　Disaffected by British insistence that they should free all their slaves, the Khamtis of Sadiya rebel: joined by the Singphos, they massacre many British officials.
1840　Third expedition against the Nagas occurs in January–February. British first become aware of the Lushais.
1841　Taghi Raja, leader of the Kapachor Akas, surrenders and persuades other Aka leaders to accept British pensions. Fourth expedition against the Nagas, winter 1841–2.
1842　The remaining Akas submit, and there are no further Aka troubles until 1883.
1843　Khamti insurrection ends, following the submission of their last leader in December. Singphos from Burma attack British outposts, and are joined by some Assamese Singphos: after their defeat many of the latter quit British territory.
1844　There is a Kuki raid on the Sylhet frontier in which 20 people are killed and six captured, resulting in a punitive British expedition in December. Fifth expedition against the Nagas occurs the same month.
1845　Sixth expedition against the Nagas.
1846　Seventh expedition against the Nagas, November 1846–January 1847. British establish an outpost at Samaguting in Angami Naga territory.
1847　First Shendu inroad into Chittagong; regular raids on Cachar, Manipur and Sylhet thereafter.
1848　First British expedition against the Abors.
1849　Eighth expedition against the Nagas sets out in November, the same month as Lushai raiders kill 29 people and capture 42.
1850　An expedition launched against the Lushais in January sees 46 Lushais killed and 429 captives freed: Lushai raids into Sylhet and Cachar cease for over a decade.

Kapachor Aka chiefs, 1847. Taghi Raja (right) and his sons Mehdi and Chandhi were the main Aka leaders with whom the British had to deal between the 1820s and 1880s. Principal Aka weapons were a bow and a 4ft (1.2m) sword, usually wielded two-handed. Their arrows were poisoned.

	Ninth expedition against the Nagas is launched in March, and the tenth in November, when 500 men with two 3-pdrs and two mortars are sent to attack Kohima, following a raid on the British outpost at Samaguting.
1851	British destroy Kohima on 11 February, killing 300 Angami Nagas: nevertheless, in the nine months following the British withdrawal in March there are 22 Naga raids (mostly in north Cachar) in which 55 people are killed, ten are wounded and 113 are captured. British outpost at Samaguting is abandoned.
1852	Second Burma War. The Garos launch seven raids between July and October, killing 44 people: a punitive expedition is mounted against them in December.
1853	In an attempt to discourage further raids, the British order that Naga affairs are 'not to be interfered with': the raids do not stop – 24 more occur between now and 1862.
1854	British establish a line of outposts along the Naga frontier.
1855	Miju Mishmis murder two French missionaries: the guilty chief is arrested by a small expedition supported by Khamti irregulars.
1856	British outpost at Dimapur on Naga frontier is abandoned.
1857	Garos launch nine raids between May 1857 and October 1859. In November Mishmi raiders massacre many Khamti women and children: the British subsequently arm the Khamtis for their own protection. On 18 November three companies of the 34th Bengal NI, stationed in Chittagong, mutiny and march through Tripura, Sylhet and Cachar, heading for Manipur. Repeatedly attacked by Kuki irregulars and detachments of the Sylhet LI en route, all but three or four are killed or captured.
1858	On 31 January a village near Dibrugarh is attacked by the Abors of

Early sketches of a Dafla warrior, a chief's widow and a chief, by John Butler. (*A Sketch of Assam*, 1847)

Kebang: 21 villagers are killed. A British expedition of 104 Assam LI and two guns sent out in March fails to take the stockade defending Kebang, runs out of supplies and is compelled to withdraw after suffering 25 per cent casualties during an Abor attack on their camp.

1859 In February the Abors advance and erect numerous stockades near Pashi: they have to be driven out by 435 British and Indian infantry and 200 irregulars, backed up by two mortars and two 12-pdrs.

1860 An inroad by 400–500 Lushais into Tripura in January is christened 'The Great Kuki Invasion'. Fifteen villages are plundered, 185 British subjects killed and 100 carried off as slaves. There is a rebellion in the Jaintia Hills against the imposition of a house tax.

1861 In January the British send a 'strong expedition' against the Thangluah Lushais, who submit. An expedition is also mounted against the Garos.

1862 An expedition of 300 Assam LI and two 12-pdr howitzers is sent against the Minyong Abors but withdraws in October when a treaty is signed promising the Abors an annual subsidy in exchange for recognising the British frontier. By 1866 the other Abor tribes have made similar agreements. Lushai raids recommence in January, with an inroad into Sylhet and the destruction of three villages, referred to as the 'Adumpur Massacre'. On 17 January another rebellion breaks out in Jaintia. A declaration of amnesty in April results in several chiefs submitting, but the last only surrenders on 9 November 1863.

1863 The Angami Nagas mount a significant raid. In May Mikir raiders from Jaintia are pursued by Frontier Police but evade capture.

1864–6 More Garo unrest is apparent.

1866 After a particularly serious raid, parts of the Garo Hills are brought under British administration. Raids cease almost immediately. A raid on a Mikir village by the Angami Nagas of Razepemah, leading to 26 deaths, results in the British razing Razepemah. Resolving to take possession of Angami territory, the British re-establish outpost at Samaguting in December. Angami raids end for a decade.

1868 Lushai raids on Naga and Kuki villages in British and Manipuri territory between October and December: the British respond with a punitive expedition.

1869 Protests regarding encroachment of tea plantations into their territory having been dismissed, Lushai raiders attack plantations in Cachar and Manipur in January and February: a British punitive expedition

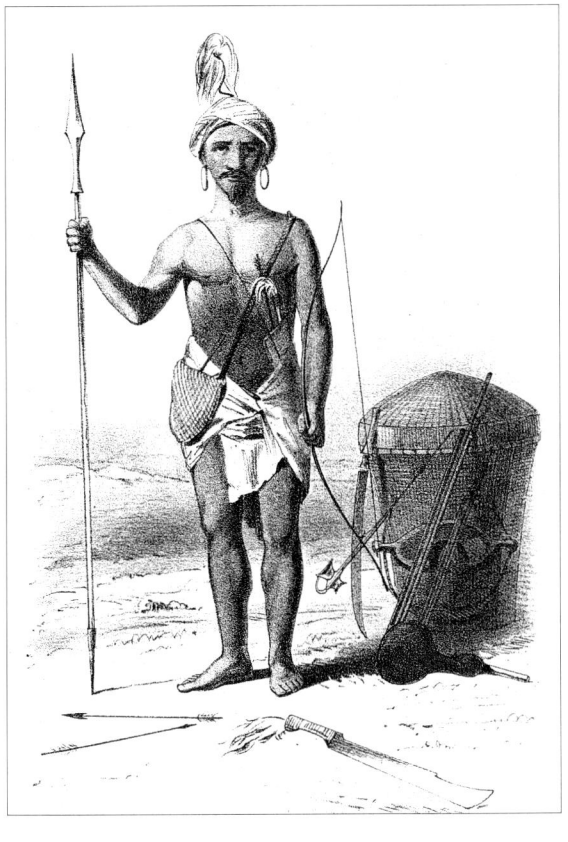

A New Kuki warrior. (John Butler, *Travels and Adventures in the Province of Assam*, 1855)

launched in February is abandoned after one of its three columns is forced back by torrential rain.

1870 First Dafla raid since 1852.

1871–2 A spate of significant Lushai raids into Manipur, Tripura and Sylhet, in which a six-year-old English girl (Mary Winchester) is seized, culminates in a 17-hour attack on a fortified tea plantation, defended by about 80 Frontier Police and sepoys: this results in a punitive expedition lasting from November 1871 to February 1872, involving 4,000 Indian troops, four mountain-guns and four mortars supported by 2,000 Manipuris. Twenty Lushai villages are destroyed and Mary Winchester is rescued. Eastern Lushai resistance is broken, and Western Lushai chiefs submit. There are no major Lushai raids for the next decade.

1872 Several Dafla raids are launched against their kinsmen settled on the plains. Attempts to carry out a census of the Garos in 1871 provoke raids which lead to the formal annexation of remaining Garo territory in winter 1872–3. Peace prevails until 1881.

1873–4 A British surveying expedition is opposed by the Nagas.

1874 Following the failure of an economic blockade (established in November 1873) designed to bring the Daflas to heel, the British launch an expedition against them in November. There are no further Dafla raids until 1887.

1875 British survey parties in the Naga Hills are opposed: one is attacked by Lhota Nagas at Wokha on 4 and 10 January: on 2 February, near Ninu, Eastern Nagas attack another party of nearly 200 men, killing its commander and 80 men and wounding another 51: these events result in a British punitive expedition in March. Lhota Naga territory is annexed and a base established at Wokha.

1876 Abors object to the presence of a British survey party in their territory: it judiciously withdraws (1877).

1877 Angami raids resume. The British respond by attacking a stronghold at Mezoma, which capitulates.

1878 British advance into the heart of Angami territory and establish an administrative headquarters at Kohima. Two small Mishmi raids occur in 1878–9: though pursued by Frontier Police the perpetrators escape.

1879 In February 50 Kukis attack a Naga village and kill 45 people. Deputy Commissioner G.H. Damant visits the Angami village of Konoma on 14 October, escorted by 21 sepoys and 65 Frontier Police. He is refused admission and shot dead with 35 of his men: another 19 are wounded. Two days later 6,000 Angamis attack the British headquarters at Kohima, which is garrisoned by about 60 men of the 43rd Assam LI and 72 Frontier Police: a reinforcement of 62 men

On the other side of the North-East Frontier the Singphos were known as Kakhyens or Kachins. This engraving of Burmese Kakhyens was prepared from a sketch drawn during the Delaporte–Garnier expedition of 1868.

Padam Abors wearing a type of cloth corselet called a *nambi*, resembling a black woollen rug worn over the head like a poncho, providing protection for the chest and back but open at the sides. Though reportedly proof against a spear-thrust, these must have had minimal defensive value. (E.T. Dalton, *Descriptive Ethnology of Bengal*, 1872)

arrives from Wokha on 19 October: Nagas suspend attacks on 24 October, when they get wind of the approach of a relief force of 2,000 Manipuris under political agent James Johnstone. The Naga forces evaporate overnight on 26–27 October, ahead of Johnstone's arrival: when a further 1,000 soldiers and Frontier Police arrive under General Nation, a punitive expedition is mounted against Konoma and a dozen other hostile villages. Konoma holds out until 22 November, when its defenders retreat to a second fortified position above the village: the British occupy or destroy six other villages.

1880   Angami fort at Konoma surrenders on 27 March, bringing the war to a close: the Angamis are fined and have to surrender their firearms. Konoma is razed and the site occupied as a British outpost.

1881   Abors move into Mishmi territory: the arrival of a British expedition deters them from crossing the Dibong River. There are Garo and Cachari rebellions, the latter resulting from a bungled British attempt to arrest a religious agitator.

1882   Lushai raids on the Chittagong frontier recommence.

1883   An expedition is launched against the Sema Nagas in June. In November a raiding party of about 100 Akas seizes three native officials in protest at government appropriation of Aka forest reserves. A British expedition of 850 men sets out on 17 December.

1884   After receiving reinforcements, the British take the main Aka village on 8 January and the captives are surrendered on 19 January: however, trouble persists, and the Aka frontier is blockaded until their leaders submit in 1888. Expeditions are mounted against the Ao or Hattigoria Nagas in July and the Sema and Ao Nagas in December 1884–January 1885.

1885–6 Third Burma War.

1886   In February 1,500 Angamis raid into Manipur: the British send an expedition against them.

1888 On 8 January 600 Lushais raid the Chengri valley, burning 24 villages, killing 101 people and carrying off 91. On 3 February a survey party is wiped out by Chins, who also raid into British territory in October. In the winter of 1888–9 a force of 200 Frontier Police enters Ao Naga territory after the Aos have requested protection against Naga tribes living beyond the Dikhu River.

1889 A British expedition against the Chins is mounted between January and May, and the chiefs responsible for the disturbances of 1888 are arrested. Though declared a success, the expedition fails to prevent Chin inroads: this, along with the renewal of Lushai raids, prompts the more significant Chin–Lushai Expedition of 1889–90, which begins in November and involves 7,400 men in three columns, one operating from Chittagong against the Lushais, the other two from Burma against the Chins. The British annex all Naga territory west of the Dikhu River.

1890 Chin and Lushai chiefs submit between January and March: British occupy Chin and Lushai territory and establish permanent outposts. Some Shendu villages are also brought under British control. The Western Lushai rebel in September but are defeated in December.

1891 In February the Southern Lushais object to the arrogance of a British official and attack his party after it has torched local rice stores: the unrest is suppressed in March. A coup in Manipur in September 1890 having been engineered by the *Senapati* (commander-in-chief), a British force of 500 men of the 42nd and 44th Gurkha LI, under James Quinton, Chief Commissioner of Assam, is sent to arrest him. Arriving at Imphal on 21 March, Quinton fails to persuade the new raja to hand over the *Senapati* and is killed, along with his senior staff, during negotiations. As a result, a substantial British expedition (4,800 men and nine guns) is despatched in April. Manipuri resistance collapses when the British enter Imphal on 27 April, and Manipur is declared forfeit to the British crown. The Angamis take advantage of the crisis in Manipur to rise against the British, but their outbreak is swiftly contained.

1892 Refusal to co-operate with the British leads to hostilities with some Eastern Lushais between February and June, following occupation of the recalcitrant chiefs' villages. Kukis massacre 286 people at Swemi/Chingjaroj, resulting in a British

Lebbey, a Heumà Shendu chief. Note his trapezoid shield, of a universal pattern found among all the Chin-Lushai peoples. Made of two or three layers of buffalo hide, these were about 2ft (60cm) long, 18in (45cm) wide at the top and 14in (35cm) at the bottom. The upper half was often decorated with four rows of brass discs and a row of red-dyed goat's hair tassels. Some substituted a single large brass disc in the centre. The colour of such shields ranged from black to very dark brown. (Sketch by S.R. Tickell, published in 1853)

An Angami Naga warrior. Round his neck he wears what later writers described as a special collar 'analogous to the military badges of rank of the civilised nations'. This comprised a piece of wood measuring 8in (20cm) by 4in (10cm) covered with rows of red and black hair and white seeds, with a fringe of red-dyed goat's hair and long black hair from the heads of his victims. (John Butler, *A Sketch of Assam*, 1847)

punitive expedition. Another expedition into the Chin Hills begins in October and lasts until March 1893. The Soktés are in rebellion until 1893.

1893 Kuki raiders massacre 300 Nagas in Manipur. In May a 100-strong British expedition burns the guilty villages and arrests their chiefs. Sokté rebels submit in August, and their chiefs are deported. Abor raids on the Miris provoke a British expedition in December, which encounters spirited opposition at Dambuk.

1894 British expedition of 100 44th Gurkha Rifles, 400 Military Police and two 7-pdr mountain-guns sets out against the Abors on 14 January, but after capturing two villages it is obliged to withdraw at the end of February when its provisions run out: the Abors harass the British withdrawal, and the expedition suffers British losses of 49 killed and 45 wounded, plus many coolies. Pasi Abor territory is blockaded thereafter until 1896, and Padam territory until 1900. The Chulikata Mishmis, also implicated in attacks on the Miris, are blockaded until 1897. Abor raids cease until 1903. Kukis attack a Tankhul Naga village, resulting in a British punitive expedition.

1895 Lushai refusal to co-operate with the British prompts an expedition which burns the offending village: the South Lushai Hills are formally annexed in September, ending Lushai resistance to British rule.

1896 Following Miri raids into their territory in January, the Apa Tanangs raid into British territory, prompting an expedition by 300 Military Police. Tankhul Nagas attack Soraphungbi village, resulting in a British punitive expedition in 1897.

1897 A murder committed in 1896 results in a 300-strong expedition against the Apa Tanangs in February. There is also an expedition against the Sema Nagas.

1899 A Bebejia Mishmi raid in May results in the murder of three Khamtis and the seizure of several children. An expedition of 120 men and two mountain-guns despatched against them in 1899–1900 razes the villages responsible and rescues the captives, but fails to arrest the perpetrators.

1900 There is a battle with Naga tribesmen on 8 February.

BRITISH FORCES ON THE NORTH-EAST FRONTIER

Although Native Infantry regiments of the East India Company (EIC) had served in Assam during the First Burma War of 1824–6, this campaign had shown that the extremes of the local climate was inimical to outsiders. Consequently the Native Infantry were withdrawn in March 1828, and the defence of the North-East Frontier was entrusted principally to three locally raised units – the Rangpur Light Infantry, the Assam *Sebundy* Corps [1] and the Sylhet Light Infantry.

The Rangpur Light Infantry had been raised at Chaubiaganj in 1817 as the Cuttack Legion. Transferred to Rangpur in 1823, it became the 10th Local or Rangpur (Local) Light Infantry Battalion, before becoming the 8th Local Battalion in 1828. Its headquarters was later moved to Bishnath, after which its men were largely recruited among Assamese hill-peoples. During the winter of 1838–9 its headquarters was transferred to Sadiya, and thence to Sibsagar by 1842. In 1844 it became the 1st Assam Light Infantry, theoretically consisting of ten companies of 100 men plus officers and NCOs.

The Assam *Sebundy* Corps, raised at Gauhati in April 1835, consisted of eight companies each of 80 men, plus officers and NCOs (or 93 men in all). Four companies consisted of *sebundies* already maintained in Assam by the previous native administration, two were newly raised, and two were transferred from the Rangpur Local Battalion. In March 1839 it was moved to Sadiya as the Assam *Sebundy* Corps (Irregulars), when its strength was increased to ten companies of 100 (plus officers and NCOs). However, this was reduced back to eight companies of 80 that August, and its name was changed to the Lower Assam *Sebundy* Corps. An Upper Assam *Sebundy* Corps of six companies was raised at Rangpur at about the same time but was disbanded in 1843. In October 1839 the Lower Assam *Sebundy* Corps was renamed the 1st Assam *Sebundy* Corps: in 1844 it became the 2nd Assam LI, with a theoretical strength of 1,000 men.

Alongside what were eventually to become the 1st and 2nd Assam LI there was the Sylhet Local Battalion. The latter had been raised as the 16th Local Battalion in February 1824, recruiting chiefly among local 'up-country' men and Manipuris. It was renumbered the 11th Local Battalion in 1826 and its headquarters was transferred to Cherrapunji in 1828, where it was to remain until 1867, when it moved to Shillong. During the early period of its existence it comprised initially eight and later ten companies of 80 men, plus officers and NCOs.

These three irregular units were transferred to the Bengal Army in 1861. The 1st Assam LI

An Angami Naga. (Sketch by Col. R.G. Woodthorpe, dated 1875)

---

1 *Sebundy* was a term used to describe irregulars utilised for police duties.

became the 46th (August–October 1861) and then the 42nd Bengal Native Infantry; the 2nd Assam LI became the 47th and then the 43rd Bengal NI; and the Sylhet LI became the 48th and then the 44th Bengal NI. Their strengths were reduced and standardised at eight companies of 89 men, comprising a *subedar*, a *jemedar*, five *havildars*, five *naiks*, two drummers and 75 privates (or 600 men, plus officers and NCOs). All three regiments underwent the first of several name changes: the 42nd and 43rd added '(Assam)' after their regimental numbers in 1885 and 1864 respectively, while the 44th added '(Sylhet)' in 1864.

Until this point these regiments had continued to draw a reasonable proportion of their men from among the local hill-peoples, but the recruitment of Gurkhas had begun at least as early as 1828, and Bengalis and Sikhs or other Punjabis were also taken on in considerable numbers. Though the enlistment of Bengalis had halted by 1880, by then the 42nd had only about 100 Assamese in its ranks: the rest were Bengalis and Sikhs. As many as half of the Sylhet LI were Gurkhas by 1854, and by 1885 the regiment was entirely Gurkha in composition. In 1880, when all three regiments had an establishment of 800 men, plus officers and NCOs (912 men in all), only the 43rd remained largely Assamese, but over the next five years Gurkhas began to predominate in the 42nd and 43rd as well as the 44th. Consequently, in 1886 they were renamed the 42nd, 43rd and 44th Gurkha LI regiments, and they became Gurkha (Rifle) Regiments in 1891.

All three served exclusively within Assam and neighbouring Burma until almost the end of the Victorian era, only serving elsewhere in India for the first time in 1899. Two battalions were customarily based at Shillong and the third at Dibrugarh, though they changed places periodically. The former provided outposts along Assam's north-east frontier and in the Naga, Khasia and Garo hills, while the latter was responsible predominantly for the Dafla, Miri and Mishmi frontiers and other points along the province's north-western frontier. During the 1870s a fourth Bengal NI regiment was generally based at Silchar, but it was withdrawn following reorganisation of the province's defences in 1881, when the Frontier Police were made responsible for all frontier outposts.

The nature of the terrain meant that no regular cavalry and few artillery were ordinarily stationed in Assam, the local detachments of mountain-artillery being reinforced from Bengal or Burma when necessary. However, two 6-pdr mountain-guns, transported by elephants, were attached to the Sylhet LI as early as 1827, and it continued to muster its own artillery section thereafter. The 42nd and 43rd were provided with guns considerably later, in 1885. The artillery of all three units was handed over to the local Military Police battalions in 1903.

Another picture of an Angami by Woodthorpe, utilising exactly the same pose as the last, but dated April 1874. It is of particular interest for the shield, covered in scarlet cloth and decorated with pieces of bearskin cut in the shape of human heads. These represented the number of heads a warrior had taken.

Sketch of a Hattigoria or Ao Naga by Woodthorpe, published in 1875.

Frontier Police and Military Police

Although army units were always on hand, and were employed in most major campaigns, their numbers were clearly insufficient to carry out the everyday patrols and minor expeditions that formed an integral part of Indian frontier management. These duties were instead left predominantly in the hands of the Frontier Police (later the Military Police) battalions, a policy doubtless motivated by economic considerations more than anything, since a police constable cost the government only Rs.180 per annum, compared to Rs.333 for a sepoy.

The Frontier Police (FP) had their origins in various irregular corps, known as 'Levies', raised during the second quarter of the 19th century. The earliest appears to have been the 600-strong Shan Levy, raised in 1825 among Shan tribesmen who had previously served with the Burmese. Initially, a quarter of them were required to serve at a time, under their own leaders, but their service strength actually fluctuated from 120 men to as many as 400. In 1831 the corps was placed under the command of a subaltern of the Sylhet LI. Gurkhas and Cacharis were subsequently recruited as being better men for hill and jungle work. Between 1846 and 1853 most of its Shans were 'retired', and by this time the corps had apparently become known as the Cachar Levy. It had meanwhile incorporated another Shan militia, the Jorhat Levy (200 men), which had been raised in 1838.

In about 1852 the Cachar Levy was split into two. One part was based at Nowgong and the other at Silchar in North Cachar. Then, when the Assamese levies were officially abolished in 1861, these two half-corps were considerably strengthened (from roughly 100–160 men to about 500–550 each) to become respectively the Nowgong Frontier Police Battalion and the North Cachar Hills Frontier Police Battalion. A 100-strong Lakhimpur Police Militia had meanwhile been established in about 1843 by the re-enlistment of men from the disbanded Upper Assam *Sebundy* Corps, and this was now reinforced in line with the two Cachar Levy corps to create a Lakhimpur Frontier Police battalion. The Nowgong unit began to be unofficially referred to as the Naga Hills Frontier Police Battalion in the mid-1860s, and this became its official title in 1872. Further reorganisation took place in 1878, by which time FP strength stood at eight inspectors, 30 sub-inspectors, 195 head constables, and 1,941 constables. These were organised into three battalions based in Assam (the Lakhimpur, Nowgong and Sibsagar battalions), responsible for 35 outposts spread over ten districts, and one battalion in neighbouring Chittagong, raised in 1871. Outposts varied greatly in size and might be manned by anything between ten and 100 men, according to circumstances.

Another militia, the Kuki Levy, was raised at Silchar in June 1850, comprising 200 Kukis and Cacharis. Opinions regarding its effectiveness seem to differ. Its men were intended to be used primarily as scouts, but, as an early commentator observed, after they had been placed under the command of the Cachar FP Battalion in 1860, 'in the endeavour to make them well drilled soldiers' they lost their 'special qualifications as scouts and trackers'. Consequently, they were amalgamated into the existing FP battalions in 1867.

Up to this point the officers of FP units were civil police inspectors and officials, but when, in 1882–3, it was decided to reconstitute the FP

A Chulikata Mishmi wearing a cane helmet with a bearskin crest and a takin-skin jacket. The latter was generally reddish brown. (E.T. Dalton, *Descriptive Ethnology of Bengal*, 1872)

as proper Military Police (MP) battalions, junior officers of the Indian Army were seconded to the new corps for terms of up to five years. The new Military Police were initially organised as four battalions, comprising the Naga Hills Battalion (headquarters Kohima), the Lakhimpur Battalion (headquarters Dibrugarh), the Cachar Battalion (headquarters Silchar), and the Surma Valley and Garo Hills Battalion (headquarters Tura). In 1882 the strength of the Naga Hills Battalion was 568 men, which later increased to 700. The Lakhimpur Battalion was also raised to 700 men in 1883, but the Garo Hills and Cachar battalions appear to have remained understrength. Two additional units – the Lungleh and Aijal battalions – were raised following the annexation of the Lushai Hills, but the Lungleh unit mutinied in August 1896, after which the two battalions were amalgamated into a single Lushai Battalion, with its headquarters at Aijal. An associated unit of about 600 men, chiefly Gurkhas and Punjabis, was raised in 1889 to guard the Chin frontier: this unit was known as the Chin Levy.

MP battalions were also established in neighbouring Burma in 1886, and these saw service in some campaigns on the North-East Frontier. By early 1888 overall MP strength in Burma stood at 13,300 of which some 5,000 were in corps conterminous with the Lushai and Chin Hills, Manipur, the Naga Hills and Singpho territory in the extreme north. In 1886 these consisted principally of the Kendat and Monywa battalions in the south (thereafter amalgamated into a single Chindwyn battalion) and in the north the Mogoung Levy, which was replaced by the Myitkhyina Battalion in 1890. The men of Burmese MP units were mostly from northern India, but each battalion generally included two or three companies of Gurkhas, and the Myitkhyina Battalion was entirely Gurkha.

HILL-TRIBES

The tribes living along India's North-East Frontier were sufficiently hostile, and their territory sufficiently impenetrable, that the British were happy to leave them alone as much as possible. Consequently, accepted practice prior to the mid-1860s was to simply despatch punitive expeditions into the hills when necessary and to establish outposts to guard particularly threatened areas. It was only the growth of the tea industry and other commercial interests in Assam that prompted the adoption of a more acquisitive policy, leading in time to the annexation of Naga, Lushai and Chin territory in particular. Nevertheless, such were the logistical difficulties of imposing British government on the region that many areas remained 'unadministered' even at the end of Victoria's reign.

As well as being inveterate raiders, the majority of the hill-peoples of Assam were also head-hunters, particularly the Garos, Kukis, Lushais and Nagas. In some isolated areas head-hunting persisted into the mid-20th century.

The Abors

The name Abors ('barbarians' or 'unfriendlies') was given to this people by the Assamese. Closely related to the Akas, Daflas and Miris, their territory lay along the Dihang River and straddled the frontier with Tibet. Their principal sub-tribes comprised the Padam (or Bor Abors), Pasi, Minyong and Galong. Each consisted of numerous independent villages thought to be capable of fielding 10,000–15,000 warriors in the 1870s. However, inter-tribal rivalries prevented them from ever putting these numbers to good effect. They had a reputation as 'the most formidable northern frontier tribe'.

First British contact with the Abors occurred in 1826, and they remained on friendly terms until the 1840s, even assisting the British during the Khamti insurrection of 1839–43. In 1847, however, the Abors attacked a party of British troops that had been sent to rescue some Cacharis seized during a raid: this resulted in the first British expedition against them the following year. After further minor confrontations and the failure of several punitive expeditions, the British adopted a conciliatory policy, and the Abors agreed to recognise the British frontier in exchange for an annual *posa* (subsidy).

Though there were no further confrontations for 30 years, the subsidy had the unintended effect of encouraging the Abors to believe that 'we were bribing them to be good neighbours because we had felt ourselves too weak to compel them to remain so'. The Padam invasion of neighbouring Mishmi territory in 1881 led to a deterioration in relations with the British, and in 1893–4 a spate of Abor raids prompted a British expedition, which was only partially successful. A blockade was then imposed on the Abor frontier and *posa* payments were discontinued. Following a general submission, sanctions against the Pasis and Minyongs were lifted in 1896, and against the Padams in 1900.

The Akas

This small tribe, numbering scarcely 1,200, won for itself a disproportionately great reputation for 'violence and audacity', to some extent as a result of its own ferocity, but more because of the influence it exerted over its far more numerous Miji neighbours and allies, 'whose countless hosts they would be able without much difficulty to lead any day against any foe'. The Mijis could muster about 5,000 men.

The Akas lived east of Bhutan. Calling themselves Hrusso (their Assamese name of 'Akas' meant 'painted', in allusion to the tattooed faces of their women), they comprised two clans known

as the Hazarikhowa ('eaters of a thousand hearths') and the Kapachors ('stealers of cotton'). The Ahom rulers of Assam had permitted them to exact an annual *posa* of pigs, fowl and silk cloth from their lowland neighbours, and the British initially adopted the same policy. However, since their tribute-collecting forays invariably degenerated into bloody raids, the British decided in 1835 to substitute a cash subsidy, thereby provoking a confused conflict which lasted until 1841. British intrusion into Aka lands to tap rubber led to further friction and border disputes, which briefly resulted in hostilities in November 1883. The only significant altercation to occur thereafter took place in 1900.

The Chins

Living in the Chin Hills, south of Manipur, these were one of a group of related peoples which Victorian commentators found it difficult to tell apart. These included the Kukis, Lushais, Pois, Shendus and Soktés, from whom the Chins differed principally in having abandoned a semi-nomadic lifestyle in favour of permanent settlements. Though the Burmese, and later the British, called them Chins (or Khyens), they called themselves Yo, Lai or Shu, and comprised a number of tribes of which the most significant were the Chinbok, Haka, Kanhow, Siyin, Tashon, Tlantlang (or Klangklang), Whenoh and Yokwa. The Tashon were the most numerous, being capable of raising 8,000–10,000 warriors, but the Siyin were the most warlike, even though they could field only about 750 men.

The frequency of their slave-raids and head-hunting forays resulted in the Chin being 'universally hated' by their neighbours, and numerous abortive expeditions were launched against the Chin from Manipur and Burma prior to British annexation of these countries. Conquest of Upper Burma finally gave the British access to the Chins' mountainous homeland at the end of the 1880s, and substantial expeditions mounted in 1889–90 and 1892–3 eventually brought them to heel. They were progressively disarmed after 1893, and the Chin Hills became a province of British Burma in 1895.

The Daflas

Living between the Akas and the Abors, the Daflas called themselves the Bangni or Nising. They were described in 1884 as 'not so much a single tribe as a collection of petty clans', but by the 1870s they were considered to comprise two principal groups, consisting of the Paschim and the Tagin, or Western Daflas and Eastern Daflas. In addition there was a sub-group known as the Apa Tanangs, living along the Kali River, of whose existence the British remained unaware until the 1870s. The Daflas and Apa Tanangs together could muster about 5,000 warriors.

Like the Akas, under Ahom rule the Daflas had been permitted to exact *posa* from the lowland tribes to their south, and the British initially continued this policy. Sporadic

LEFT ABOVE **Kuki chief wearing one of the decorated turbans by which they could be distinguished from other tribesmen. (E.T. Dalton, *Descriptive Ethnology of Bengal*, 1872)**

LEFT BELOW **Soibang Vangam, an Eastern Naga chief. (Sketch by Woodthorpe, published in 1875)**

BELOW **Tankhul Nagas. Note the distinctive way in which the sides of the head were shaved to leave a ridge of hair on the scalp. In 1891 Ethel Grimwood described this as giving them 'the appearance of cockatoos'. The Tankhuls were the southern division of the Luhupa tribe, who were found in North-East Manipur. (John Butler, *A Sketch of Assam*, 1847)**

Dafla raids occurred from 1835, leading to the British suspending their right to collect *posa*, but in 1852 they subsided following the establishment of a line of outposts along the Dafla frontier. No further trouble occurred until the 1870s: following several raids on villages in British territory and the failure of an economic blockade, a punitive expedition was despatched against them in the winter of 1874–5. Minor raids punctuated the 1880s and 1890s, and Dafla tribesmen were still seizing travellers and frontier workers even in 1900.

The Garos

Calling themselves the Mandé, the most important of their dozen or so sub-tribes were the Abeng, Atong, Awé and Machi. They were a warlike people who could probably muster about 15,000 warriors and had a deserved reputation for head-hunting and slave-raiding (as much as 40 per cent of the population consisted of slaves). They were responsible for numerous destructive raids into British territory throughout the 1840s and 1850s, launching as many as seven raids in 1852 alone. This eventually resulted in the British imposing their jurisdiction on about 100 Garo villages between 1866 and 1871, though about 60 more maintained their independence until 1872. Following several 'murderous raids' that year, three detachments of Frontier Police were sent into the hills. The Garos were defeated, and their territory was annexed.

Galong (or Doba) Abor. He wears the usual 'war-coat', and his cane helmet is decorated with boar's tusks. (E.T. Dalton, *Descriptive Ethnology of Bengal*, 1872)

The Jaintias and Khasias

The Khasias referred to their Jaintia cousins as Sintengs, but the British frequently referred to both peoples as Khasias or Khasis. They had established numerous petty states in what were known as the Khasia and Jaintia Hills. Their chiefs were originally permitted a large measure of autonomy, but the lands of the Khasias proper were occupied following an uprising in 1829–33, and the powers of their chiefs were whittled away.

Jaintia was the most significant Khasia state, being a confederation of about 25 smaller chieftainships under a paramount chief, generally referred to as the Raja of Jaintia. The penultimate raja, Ram Singh II (1789–1832), had acknowledged allegiance to the Britain in March 1824 and sent troops to support the British during the First Burma War. A dispute over frontiers in the aftermath of this conflict eventually led to the British annexing Jaintia in 1835, deposing Raja Indra Singh (1832–5). The exiled raja was later suspected of complicity in the rebellions that erupted in Jaintia in 1860 and 1862–3. The 1860 rebellion was nipped in the bud, but the second outbreak saw 15 months of bitter fighting before order was finally restored.

The Khasias proper could muster a total of about 16,000 warriors, and a handful of their individual chiefs could field 2,000–3,000 men each in the 1830s. However, Jaintia could probably raise only about 4,000.

The Khamtis

The Khamtis consisted of a few thousand Shans living in the Sadiya district. The British considered them the most civilised of all the mountain tribes in Assam, but this admiration was not mutual: a British commentator noted that the Khamtis had 'a greater respect for Burma than for us, and imagine Burma stronger than we are'. Indeed, the Khamtis were still sending presents to the King of Burma in the 1880s.

When the British occupied Assam during the First Burma War they acknowledged the Khamti raja – known by the Ahom title of *Sadiya Khowa Gohain* – as 'local officer of the Assam government', expecting him to maintain 200 men on behalf of the EIC thereafter. However, following his death in 1835 the British deposed his son and installed a political agent. In 1839 an insurrection began with an attack on the British base at Sadiya. The Khamtis maintained the struggle until 1843, possibly with clandestine Burmese support, but there were no further hostilities thereafter.

The Kukis

As a result of increasing populations and inter-tribal hostilities, the Kukis, Lushais, Chins and other related tribes were gradually driven north during the 18th and 19th centuries. The name Kuki first occurs in British sources in 1792, though prior to 1871–2 (when 'Lushai' began to be substituted) they used it as a generic term to describe all hill-men who descended on the frontiers of Tripura and Cachar from the south-east.

The Kukis proper were a semi-nomadic people consisting of the Naia, or New Kukis, and the Purama, or Old Kukis. The latter had been driven

A group of Miju Mishmis photographed in the 1870s.

An Eastern Naga in typical cane helmet and tight cane girdle. One report describes how they 'took a special pride in reducing the waist to an amazingly small size by pulling the cane as tight as was endurable'. (E.T. Dalton, *Descriptive Ethnology of Bengal*, 1872)

into Cachar and Manipur in considerable numbers during the late 18th century, and by the Victorian period there were probably about 5,000 in Cachar and 11,000 in Manipur, divided into more than a dozen clans, of which the most significant were the Bete and Khelma in Cachar, and the Kom in Manipur. The New Kukis constituted a second wave of invaders who in the 1840s and 1850s were driven north on the heels of the Old Kukis by the Lushais, Soktés and Pois to their rear. Consequently they were often at war with the Old Kuki clans who stood in their way, particularly the Kom, but the British nevertheless permitted them to settle in Cachar. There were four principal New Kuki clans, of which the Thado were by far the most important. Their total population was probably 35,000–40,000 during the closing decades of Queen Victoria's reign: they were found mostly in Manipur but were also scattered through North Cachar and the Naga Hills.

The Kukis raided the Cachar, Tripura and Chittagong frontiers almost continuously from the late 18th century, but most such raids attributed to the Kukis after about 1850 were actually the work of Lushais.

The Lushais

Moving steadily north and driving the Kukis before them, from the mid-19th century the Lushais occupied the entire region between Cachar in the north, Tripura and Chittagong in the west and the territory of the Soktés and Pois in the east. Semi-nomadic, inveterate raiders and traditional enemies of the Nagas, they called themselves the Zo or Mizo ('people' or 'hill-people'). The most important of their dozen or more clans were the Howlongs, the Syloos and the Thangluahs (sometimes referred to by the British as the Rutton-Poeas), whose respective populations by the 1870s were roughly 12,500, 11,000 and 2,600. The total Lushai population was estimated at 60,000–80,000.

The Syloos were the most powerful clan, and it was the dynasty established in the 1850s by their chief Lalulla which ruled most of the Lushai Hills district until it was annexed by the British towards the end of the 19th century. The clans ruled by the descendants of his sons Bhuta and Mungpira were referred to respectively as the Eastern and Western Lushais. The Howlongs, with whom the Syloos were frequently at odds, ruled much of the southern Lushai Hills, while Thangluah territory adjoined the Chittagong Hill Tracts. Though the Thangluahs submitted to the British at the beginning of the 1860s (only to be destroyed by the Shendus a decade later), the other clans raided Manipur, Tripura and Sylhet continually from the mid-19th century, and it was the intensification of these raids in 1870–1 that resulted in the British expedition against them in 1871–2. Several further British expeditions between 1889 and 1895 ended with the complete subjugation of the Lushai Hills.

The Mikirs

The Mikirs called themselves the Ar-leng ('men'). They were found in North Cachar, the Jaintia Hills and the Mikir Hills. Beyond occasional family or village vendettas among themselves, they were considered 'the most peaceful and industrious of the hill tribes', and consequently they suffered severely at the hands of their Angami Naga neighbours. They came under British jurisdiction in 1838, and on only one occasion thereafter was it necessary for an expedition of Frontier Police to be sent against them, following an attack on a rival Mikir village in May 1863. They are estimated to have numbered about 60,000 in the 1870s and about 90,000 by the end of the century. Their dress was similar to the Khasias, and like the Khasias they frequently served as porters during British expeditions into the hills.

The Miris

This was the Assamese name of a semi-nomadic people who called themselves Mishings and were found scattered throughout Upper Assam and the extreme south-east of Tibet. They were considered an offshoot of the Abors: 'the Abors look upon the Miris as their dependants, and used to demand a heavy tribute from them, to escape which numbers of the latter flocked into British territory', noted one contemporary. The British were able to maintain friendly relations with them from the outset, perhaps because they posed no military threat. They resembled the Daflas.

The Mishmis

The Mishmis occupied the extreme north-east corner of the North-East Frontier, beyond the Dibang River, wedged in on three sides by Tibet, China and Burma and having the Abors for neighbours to the west. Their four main tribes were the Bebejia, Chulikata, Digaru and Miju. The Chulikata, or 'crop-haired Mishmis', were reputedly the most warlike, being described in the 1870s as 'annually carrying fire and sword into the country of their neighbours, the Digaru and Miju Mishmis, by whom they are both feared and detested'. However, all the Mishmi tribes were fairly militant, and as early as 1847 they are recorded to have been 'constantly engaged in petty wars among themselves and their neighbours, the Abors and Singphos'. The Abors invaded western Mishmi territory in 1881, forcing the British to establish an outpost of 300 Frontier Police at Nizamghat.

British hostilities against them began with a punitive expedition following the murder of two French missionaries returning from Tibet in 1855. Raids increased in intensity thereafter, and in 1866 the British

Luhupa Nagas from Manipur. The left-hand figure wears a military jacket, possibly indicating he is a Manipuri regular soldier. The Luhupas wore distinctive cane helmets, which invariably had a large brass cymbal in front (*luhup* is the Manipuri word for helmet). The one depicted here also has red-dyed plumes at each side and a bearskin chin-strap. (Ethel Grimwood, *My Three Years in Manipur*, 1891)

supplied arms to the local Khamtis to defend themselves against the Mishmis. This proved so successful that there was little further trouble beyond minor raids in 1878–79, 1893 and 1899.

The Nagas

Regarded by some Victorian commentators as constituting 'the wildest and most turbulent tribes adjacent to any part of our Indian dominions', the Nagas inhabited the hills that separated Assam from North-West Burma. The most important of their 40 or so tribes were the Angamis, Aos, Kachas, Lhotas, Rengmas, Semas and numerous small tribes referred to collectively as the Eastern or Naked Nagas, or Konyaks. Naga tribes varied in size from one up to several dozen sizeable villages – the Semas, for instance, held five villages, and the Angamis at least 80. Each tribe was capable of raising between about 100 and 800 warriors. Calculations of their overall population suggest that in the 1880s there may have been about 120,000 in the Naga Hills, plus another 30,000–40,000 in Manipur and 6,000 in Tripura, implying an overall military potential of perhaps 30,000–35,000 men. However, an estimate of 1855 put the population of just two tribes – the Angamis and Kachas – at 125,000, so clearly such figures must be treated with caution. What is certain is that during 1879–80 the Angamis alone (admittedly the largest Naga tribe) fielded some 8,000 men.

This photograph of Eastern Naga artefacts, published in 1898 but probably taken in the 1880s, includes two helmets, a chief's ceremonial hair extension (right), and a hide corselet. Armour was rare among the Nagas. This example is basically the same as the Kuki corselet portrayed in Plate E.

Although they had maintained friendly relations with the Ahom rulers of Assam, their predilection for raiding inspired fear and hatred in all their other neighbours. Naga raids into the Nowgong and Sibsagar districts in the north and Cachar in the south-west commenced soon after British occupation of the province began. The Angamis were soon found to be the most warlike tribe, and most of the subsequent British military activity was directed against them. This went through three distinct phases: between 1832 and 1850 frequent punitive expeditions were launched in an effort to halt raids into British territory; between 1851 and 1865 a policy of non-intervention was adopted; and finally, after 1866, a concerted drive towards annexation and control of all Naga territory steadily gained momentum. The less warlike tribes capitulated gladly, looking to the British to protect them from the raids of more aggressive neighbours, but others (notably the Angamis and Lhotas) resisted ferociously. The conflict reached its climax in 1879–80, with the Angami siege of Kohima and the retaliatory British siege of Konoma, which broke the back of (though it did not end) Angami resistance. Sporadic Naga raids continued well into the 20th century.

The Pois

The name Poi seems to have been adopted as a collective term to describe numerous small tribes, also referred to as Chillongs, who were

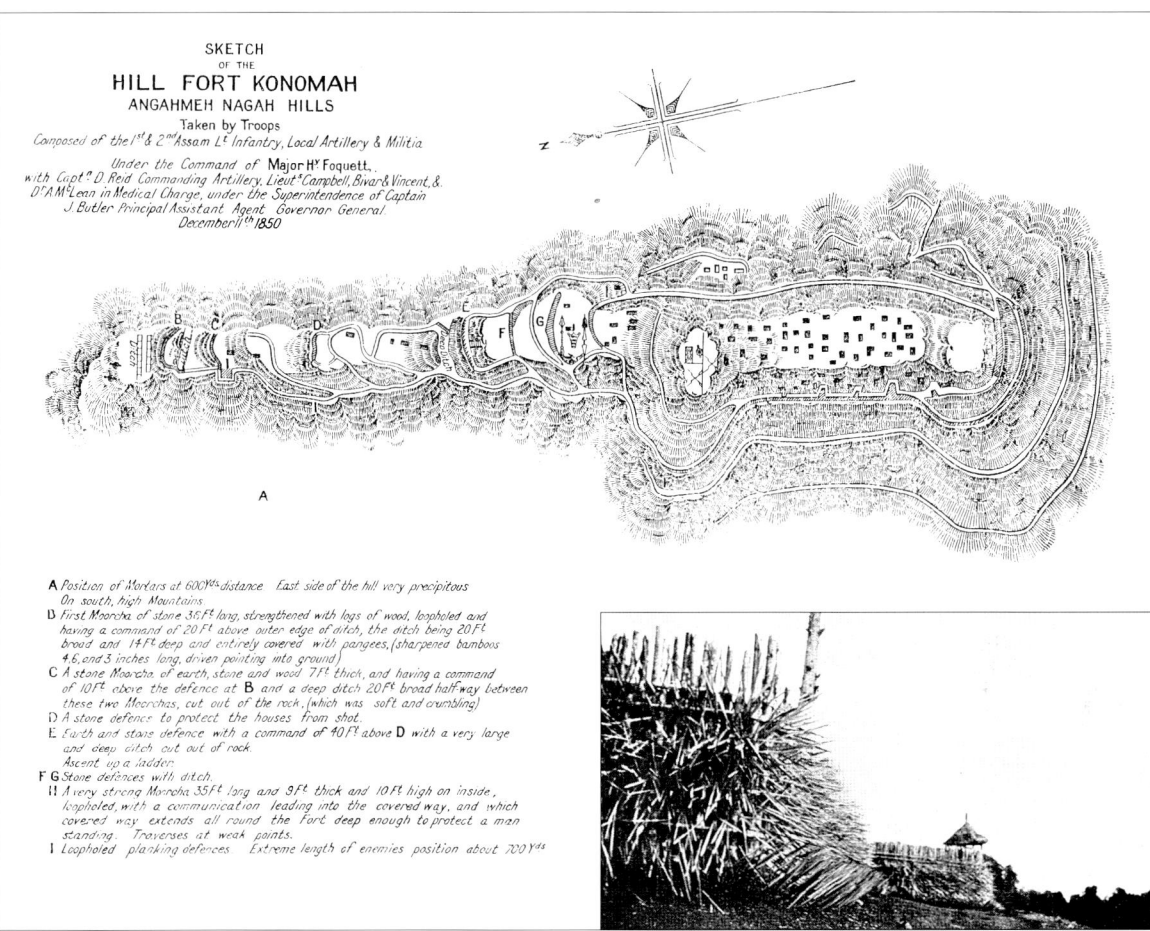

A contemporary sketch-map of the sophisticated Angami fortifications encountered by the British at Konoma in December 1850.

INSET Bamboo spikes, or *panjis*, were widely used in the defence of villages and fortified sites throughout the North-East Frontier. This is a Frontier Police post at Mongsemdi in the Naga Hills. (L.W. Shakespear, *History of the Assam Rifles*, 1929)

apparently closely related to the Chins. They lived east and south of the Howlong Lushais, to the east of the Koladyne River. Their cumulative military potential was rumoured to be sizeable, and was certainly sufficient for them to be exerting considerable pressure on the Lushais by about 1850. However, they seem to have suffered continually at the hands of their Sokté kinsmen, perhaps because by 1875 two-thirds of the latter were reputedly armed with muskets.

The Shendus

The Shendus dwelt along the Koladyne River on the borders of Arracan. They were often confused with the Chins or the Pois, probably being related to both. In 1846 one British officer described them as the most powerful tribe on the Koladyne: 'The suddenness, secrecy and never-failing nature of [their] attacks cause them to be held, by the rest, in a dread of which it would be impossible to give an idea.' They were responsible for driving the Lushais north and west during the first half of the 19th century, and they raided repeatedly into Chittagong until the 1890s. They continued to persecute the Lushais in the 1870s and 1880s, utterly destroying the Thangluah clan in about 1873. There are no worthwhile contemporary calculations of their numerical strength, but it must have been considerable.

Some Shendu territory came into British hands as a result of the

A stone wall at Jotsoma, typical of those which subdivided Naga villages to protect individual clans from one another. Such defences could be several metres thick.

Abor example of a favourite defensive device among Assamese hill-peoples, the 'stone shoot'. It consisted of a bamboo platform piled with stones, erected on the hillside above a path along which it was anticipated the enemy would come. The platform would be released by a trip-line, or the ropes would be cut with a *dao*, tipping an avalanche of boulders on to the heads of the enemy. Despite the fact that the underbrush was generally cleared to give the descending stones a clear run, 'stone shoots' were apparently not easy to see from below. However, the British became accustomed to despatching flanking parties specifically to seek them out. (Sachin Roy, *Abor Weapons of War and Chase*, 1956)

Chin-Lushai expedition of 1889–90, but the rest remained unadministered until as late as 1930, with head-hunting raids continuing well into the 1920s.

The Singphos

Often called 'Chingpaws' by the British, the Singphos were related to the Khamtis. They appear to have comprised about a dozen main tribes which had established themselves on both sides of the Patkoi range separating Upper Burma from Assam following the Burmese invasion of 1818. They were accused of depopulating entire districts by their slave-raids. During the First Burma War they fought for the Burmese, but 16 of their 28 chiefs submitted to the British in 1826.

However, raids sputtered on, and in 1843 hostilities erupted on a grand scale, prompted by the fact that the British had forbidden the Singphos to own slaves, thus leaving them unable to cultivate their lands. The Singphos overwhelmed the outpost at Bisa, but attacks on two other posts were beaten off, and after several months of fighting the chiefs surrendered. Many Singphos subsequently left Assam and returned to the Hukong Valley, beyond the frontier of British-administered territory. There were no further conflicts, and in the second half of the 19th century the Singphos proved of considerable value to the British in curbing the worst excesses of the local Naga tribes. They were thought to be capable of raising 9,000–10,000 men.

1. Angami Naga warrior
2. Eastern Naga warrior
3. Lhota Naga warrior

1. Abor warrior
2. Abor warrior
3. Abor chieftain

1. Khamti warrior
2. Garo warrior
3. Khasia warrior

1. Dafla warrior
2. Singpho warrior
3. Mishmi *gam*

1. Kuki warrior
2. Lushai warrior
3. Chin warrior

1. Kuki or Lushai chief
2. Shendu warrior
3. Manipuri sepoy

1. Sylhet Light Infantry, 1837
2. 44th Bengal Native Infantry, 1875
3. Sema Naga in British service

1. Frontier Police, c. 1848–68
2. Frontier Police, 1868–85
3. Military Police, 1885–1901

The Soktés

These were also referred to as Sooties, Paités (or Pytoos), Pallians and Kamhows. Victorian sources variously classify them as being a Chin or Lushai people, and while they were probably related to both, they appear to have had a stronger connection with the former than the latter. They could field 2,000 warriors in the 1880s. Their territory straddled the Manipuri-Burmese border, but they were being steadily driven north-west by the Shendus, and were in turn driving the Lushais and Pois before them. They raided into Manipur from the 1850s until at least the end of the 1870s, launching nine sizeable forays there between 1857 and 1871 and prompting retaliatory Manipuri expeditions, notably in 1857 and 1875. They also raided in Burma in 1878, and the Burmese responded with an expedition of 2,000 men. After about 1880 many began to settle as agriculturists in Manipur.

MANIPUR

Comprising some 8,000 square miles of hill-country surrounding a central valley wherein lay the capital Imphal, this was the only native power of any significance on the North-East Frontier following British annexation of Assam and Cachar. Its population was estimated at between 50,000 and 180,000 Meitheis (Manipuris) plus some 80,000–110,000 Nagas and Kukis, who spent much of their time raiding each other. Following the First Burma War the British had recognised Gambhir Singh as raja in 1826. He was succeeded in 1834 by his infant son Chandra Kirti Singh, who was temporarily displaced in 1844–50 by the regent Nar Singh. However, Chandra was reinstated following the death of Nar and the flight of Nar's brother Debendra. Disturbances instigated by Debendra and his kinsmen sputtered on until as late as 1866, and from about 1845 the country also suffered from numerous New Kuki, Naga, Lushai and Sokté raids, which frequently left its defences in disarray. In addition there were occasional border clashes with the Burmese.

Chandra Kirti reigned from 1850 to 1886 and was succeeded by his son Sura Chandra. However, in March 1890 Sura was deposed by his half-brother Kula Chandra at the instigation of another half-brother, the *Senapati* (army commander-in-chief) Koireng Tikendrajit Bir Singh. Sura appealed to the British for help, but they opted to recognise Kula as raja while at the same time despatching a force of 500

A good picture of Abor warriors, demonstrating the diversity of their costumes. The left-hand figure wears a knee-length *nambi*, while the man in the middle wears a *perding galuk* – see Plate B. (L.W. Shakespear, *History of the Assam Rifles*, 1929)

LEFT **A romantic picture of Dafla 'scouts' from the *Illustrated London News* of 27 March 1875, based on a sketch by John Butler Jr. The tattoos on their cheeks indicate that these are Eastern Daflas. However, there are various aspects of their costume that the London-based engraver has failed to understand, not least the arrangement of their hair and the cane hoops round their bodies.**

RIGHT **Elements of the 44th Bengal NI crossing a tributary of the Brahmaputra during the Dafla expedition of 1874–5. This engraving conveys some idea of the terrain encountered on such expeditions. (*Illustrated London News*, 20 February 1875)**

men to remove the *Senapati*, who was regarded as a threat to the region's stability. After failing to arrest the *Senapati* the British mission's senior staff were all murdered during negotiations with the raja, leading to the Manipur War of 1891. Manipur was declared forfeit to the British crown following the occupation of Imphal, although this order was rescinded in September, when Nar Singh's great-grandson Chura Chand Singh was installed as raja. Kula Chandra and the *Senapati* had meanwhile both been captured by the British: the former was deported, the latter executed.

The Manipuri army

Traditionally Manipur had raised its armed forces through a militia levy known as the *lal-up*, which called for military service from all men aged 16–60 for ten days in every 40 in rotation. However, during the 1820s a more conventional regular army had come into existence following the organisation by the British in 1823 of a 500-strong contingent of Manipuris to assist in driving the Burmese out of Cachar. In 1825 this all-infantry force was increased to 2,000 men, placed under two British officers, and became the Manipur Levy, paid and armed by the British government. British financial support of the levy was withdrawn in 1835, however, as were the British officers, but the EIC continued to provide its arms and ammunition. It was later increased to 3,000 men through the old *lal-up* system. About 400 men served for a year at a time, receiving grants of land in lieu of payment. By 1879 its strength had grown to an estimated 5,000–6,000 men, and ten years later it stood between 6,200 and 7,000 men. According to British commentators this force was poorly trained, ill-disciplined, and over-supplied with incompetent officers. The British, in fact, considered the Kuki irregulars who served alongside the regular Manipuri army on most occasions as superior in every way to the latter.

Specific details of unit organisation are unknown, but there appear to have been eight regiments, each consisting of between eight and 12 companies. Regiments were commanded by majors, and companies by *subedars*. There are indications that regimental strength was between 400 and 800 men, but the size of individual companies is not recorded. There was also a small amount of artillery: four 7-pdr rifled mountain-guns, eight 3-pdr smoothbores, two 2-pdrs, and a 4½-in mortar were captured by the British at Imphal in 1891.

The Manipuri army acted in support of the British on several occasions, notably during the Lushai expedition of 1871–2 (2,000 men), for the relief of Kohima in 1879 (2,000 men) and in the Kebaw Valley in 1886, during the Third Burma War (800 men). It was disarmed and disbanded by the British in 1891.

WARFARE ON THE NORTH-EAST FRONTIER

Very few of the local hill-peoples ever attempted to meet the British in the open field, and of those that did, even fewer attempted to do so again once they had experienced the destructive powers of British artillery and disciplined musketry. A battle against the Angamis near Kekrima in 1851 was one of the exceptions: the Nagas suffered 300 casualties in what boiled down to a few minutes of fighting. Most warfare in the region therefore involved ambushes and night-attacks by the hill-peoples – enabling them to make best use of the terrain and their local knowledge – while British expeditions largely involved assaults on the fortified villages and stockades in which the enemy took refuge.

Most campaigning by either side took place during the cold weather that commenced at the end of the year. The summer months – lasting roughly from May to September – were a period of sweltering heat and torrential rain which caused extensive flooding and rendered rivers impassable. In most areas only the months of October to February were sufficiently dry and tolerably cool for raids or military expeditions.

Raids by the hill-peoples generally involved a night-march to the vicinity of a target village or plantation, which would only be attacked if the enemy could be taken completely unawares: the assault would be made about an hour before dawn. Often the village was set alight and the inhabitants massacred or captured as they fled. Gathering their loot and prisoners, they would then withdraw at such a pace (utilising animal trails and the courses of small streams) that there was

A Frontier Police outpost typical of the masonry variety built in the 1830s. This is Dikrang post, near Sadiya, which remained in use until 1900. (L.W. Shakespear, *History of the Assam Rifles*, 1929)

no chance of regular troops catching up with them. Pursuit was further hindered by the raiders sewing the paths behind them with *panjis*, bamboo spikes varying between a few inches and three or four feet in length. When hidden in long grass, these were difficult to see, and men running on to them were severely or even fatally wounded.

Ambushes involved attacking regular troops on the march. The hill-peoples would wait silently for hours, concealed in the foliage below the path along which the British column would have to pass. As it went by, they would fire off a single volley of arrows or musketry before decamping down the hillside at speed. Then, a short way further on, the whole process would be repeated. A British column struggling along in single file and unable to send out flanking detachments because of the terrain was extremely vulnerable to such attacks. The ambushers would 'buzz about the long unwieldy column like hornets, firing first into the advance guard, then into the baggage, and again into the rearguard'. Returning fire achieved little, since a hill-man in his own terrain was, as one officer remarked, the 'most difficult enemy to see or hit I ever saw'. Similar tactics were adopted at river-crossings or at any point where the column had to negotiate some natural obstacle. Camp sites were also harried under cover of darkness.

The path might also be booby-trapped. Deep pit-falls concealed beneath twigs and leaves, shallow holes lined with poisoned *panjis*, wayside trees hacked through and ready to fall at the slightest touch, trip-lines designed to release volleys of poisoned arrows, or avalanches of stones from 'stone shoots' were the most widespread of the horrors that awaited unwary assailants.

Hill-villages were invariably defended. The Nagas and Singphos, and from about the mid-19th century the Kukis and Lushais too, constructed

A Gurkha of the Frontier Police, photographed in 1877. Though they wore their full uniform when in barracks, at this date the uncomfortable European boots and trousers were often abandoned once men were in the field.

strong stockades around their villages, sometimes involving several lines of *panjis*, earth and bamboo palisades and ditches: the defences of some Angami villages even included thick stone walls and squat towers. The Shendus erected a fort in the centre of the village instead, and the Abors, Akas, Chins and Daflas built one or more stockades on high ground commanding the approaches, leaving the village itself unguarded except for slight defences protecting its gates. Entrances consisted of heavy timber doors, usually at the end of a narrow, sunken path between high banks topped by tangled brambles, or accessible only by means of a ladder or a single narrow plank over a *panji*-spiked ditch.

On occasion the fortifications were substantial enough to withstand artillery fire: mountain-guns had minimal effect on a stone-faced Angami earthwork at Konoma in 1850, for instance, or on the Abor stockade at Dambuk in 1894. Nevertheless, their stockades had weaknesses. They were particularly susceptible to attacks from above, but the siting of most rendered turning movements impossible, while ditches, *panjis* and the very narrowness of the approaches made escalades difficult. Unsurprisingly, therefore, it was in the defence of fortified sites that hill-peoples were potentially at their most dangerous, and they would resolutely stand to their defences until the moment that an assault was pressed home; then they would swiftly decamp from the rear. Even where the defenders successfully withstood an assault, they usually took the opportunity of darkness to slip away at the end of the first day's fighting, albeit sometimes only as far as a second line of defences.

In attacking stockades, the British would weaken the defences with their mountain-guns where they could, before sending in a storming party which was given covering fire from the flanks. The enemy would customarily flee as the storming party approached, enabling the British to hack their way through the *panjis* and stockade with their kukris. Unsurprisingly, on those occasions where the enemy did not run, such a brash assault was invariably repulsed.

A sergeant of the Chittagong Frontier Police Battalion in summer uniform, 1882. Though this was nominally white, the photograph seems to indicate that it was dyed a pale shade of khaki. He is armed with a Snider rifle and kukri. (Emil Riebeck, *The Chittagong Hill-Tribes*, 1885)

FURTHER READING

Barpujari, H.K. *Assam in the Days of the Company 1826–1858* (1963)
Butler, John *A Sketch of Assam* (1847)
Butler, John *Travels and Adventures in the Province of Assam* (1855)
Carey, Bertram S. and Tuck, H.N. *The Chin Hills* (1896)
Chakravorty, B.C. *British Relations with the Hill Tribes of Assam since 1858* (1964)
Elwin, Verrier *India's North-East Frontier in the Nineteenth Century* (1959)
Elwin, Verrier *The Nagas in the Nineteenth Century* (1969)
Frontier and Overseas Expeditions from India Volumes IV–V (1907)
Gait, Edward A. *A History of Assam* (1906)
Grimwood, Ethel St. Clair *My Three Years in Manipur* (1891)
Hunter, W.W. *The Statistical Account of Assam* (1879)
Hutton, J.H. *The Angami Nagas* (1922)
Huxford, H.J. *History of the 8th Gurkha Rifles 1824–1949* (1952)
Johnstone, James *My Experiences in Manipur and the Naga Hills* (1896)
Lewin, Thomas H. *A Fly on the Wheel* (1912)
MacCall, Anthony *Lushai Chrysalis* (1949)
Mackenzie, Alexander *History of the Relations of the Government with the Hill Tribes of the North-East Frontier of Bengal* (1884)
Military Report on the Chin-Lushai Country (1893)
Osik, N.N. *British Relations with the Adis 1825–1947* (1992)
Parratt, John and S.N.A. *Queen Empress vs Tikendrajit Prince of Manipur: The Anglo–Manipuri Conflict of 1891* (1992)
Reid, A.S. *Chin-Lushai Land* (1893)
Robinson, William *A Descriptive Account of Assam* (1841)
Shakespear, J. *The Lushei Kuki Clans* (1912)
Shakespear, L.W. *History of Upper Assam, Upper Burma and North-Eastern Frontier* (1914)
Shakespear, L.W. *History of the Assam Rifles* (1929)
Shaw, William *The Thadou Kukis* (1929)
Stewart, R. 'Notes on Northern Cachar', *Journal of the Asiatic Society of Bengal* XXIV (1855)
Waddell, L.A. 'The Tribes of the Brahmaputra Valley', *Journal of the Asiatic Society of Bengal* LXIX (1901)
Woodthorpe, R.G. *The Lushai Expedition* (1873)
Woodthorpe, R.G. 'Notes on the Wild Tribes Inhabiting the So-called Naga Hills on our North-East Frontier of India', *Journal of the Anthropological Institute* XI (1882)

Men of the Lakhimpur Frontier Police Battalion photographed in 1887. Despite its conversion into a Military Police unit in 1882-3, this battalion retained its old 'Frontier Police' title until 1888. (L.W. Shakespear, *History of the Assam Rifles*, 1929)

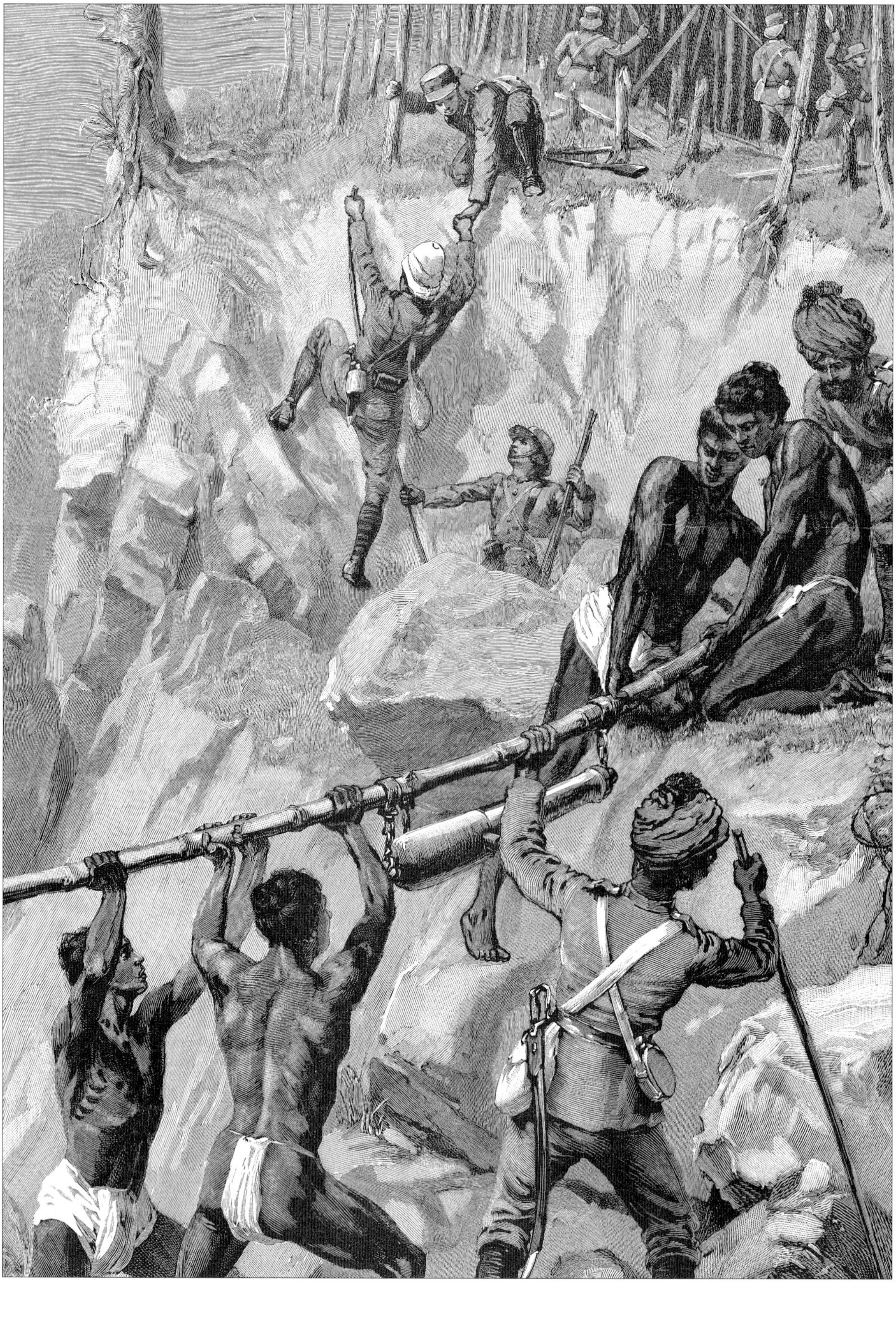

THE PLATES

A1. ANGAMI NAGA WARRIOR
The universal Naga weapon was the spear, with a bamboo shaft, a long, leaf-shaped iron blade, and a pointed iron ferrule. Overall length could be up to about 8ft (2.4m). The shaft was either plain or ornamented with red-dyed goat's hair, with a space sometimes left bare for the hand. The Naga customarily carried two spears; a plain, shorter one for throwing, and the longer, decorated one for use at close quarters. Secondary armament consisted of the hatchet-like *dao*, often described as a P-shaped axe. This had a blade of about 9in (23cm) which was 4in (10cm) wide at the tip, narrowing to an inch (25mm) at the base. It was carried in a wooden block suspended behind the right buttock.

Angami shields were 5–7ft (1.5–2.1m) long and 2–2½ft (60–75cm) wide at the top, narrowing to about 18in (45cm) at the bottom. They were made of bamboo matting covered on the outside with elephant, tiger, leopard, deer, buffalo, bear or rhinoceros skin. At their most elaborate they were decorated with a long cane projecting from each upper corner, supporting tufts of human and dyed goat's hair; in the centre of the top edge was a tall plume of goat's hair; and at the back edge a row of feather tassels.

A2. EASTERN NAGA WARRIOR
In Victorian times the Eastern Naga were often known as 'Naked Nagas' because they did not wear loincloths. (It was only under British influence in the 1870s that loincloths started to be adopted.) They shaved their heads up to the crown, but grew their hair long behind and tied it up in a bun. This man wears the very tight cane or bark waistband popular among some Eastern Naga tribes, drawn so tight that the waist was reduced 'to a very small compass'. Many Eastern Nagas also tattooed themselves quite extensively.

Helmets were a characteristic feature of their costume. They were conical, made of plaited cane, and were either plain or had patterns of coloured straw worked over them. Boar's tusks were attached to each side, and a large plume of black or red-dyed hair sometimes traversed the crown from front to back. A single small black feather, or a larger toucan feather, usually stood erect from the top of the crown. Their ridged, rectangular shields were 3–4ft (0.9–1.2m) long and 1½–2ft (45–60cm) wide, made of buffalo hide and painted black.

A3. LHOTA NAGA WARRIOR
Note the fairly rigid separate cloth apron covering the front of his black loincloth. This was also black, about 14in (35cm) deep by 12in (30cm) wide and profusely decorated with close-set rows of cowrie shells or little white seeds. He also wears a fringed baldric across his chest from the right shoulder, which supports a 'tail' behind the small of his back. This tail was basically an 18in (45cm) extension of the *panji* quiver often worn by Naga warriors. It was made of wood and decorated with scarlet-dyed goat's hair or long tresses of black hair taken from the bodies of women the Nagas had killed in their raids.

The Lhota *dao* differed somewhat from the more typical variety such as was carried by the Angamis. It usually had a 12in (30cm) blade that was up to 5in (12.5cm) wide at the top and 1½in (38mm) wide at the bottom, with both the edge and the back slightly curved.

B1 & B2. ABOR WARRIORS
Figure B1 wears just a bark-fibre *suria* (loincloth) supported by a few rings of cane round the waist. The apron hangs down in front in loose strips about 15in (37.5cm) long, sometimes described as looking like 'a white bushy beard'. His only other article of dress is a hat which in wartime doubled as a helmet. This was most often made of tightly woven basketwork, with a stout brim and a crown strengthened by additional strips of cane. In combat it was secured by means of a chin-strap. Note the satchel carried at the hip, which contained a warrior's pipe, tobacco, betel and the like. Provisions and other items of equipment were carried in a rucksack like those of the Daflas on page 34. In addition to a loincloth, B2 wears a short-sleeved waistcoat and a short, thick, coarse woollen corselet called a *perding galuk*, with a high collar to protect the neck.

The most characteristic Abor weapons were bow and arrows and either a short, one-edged *dao* or a long, straight sword of Tibetan origin. Their arrows – carried in a bamboo quiver which had a lid and an outside 'pocket' – were poisoned with a mixture of aconite and croton berries. Most

LEFT **This picture, sketched during the Chin-Lushai expedition, demonstrates the enormous difficulties faced in moving artillery on the North-East Frontier. It was transported by elephants as far as possible, but usually ended up being carried by coolies. (*Illustrated London News*, 1 April 1893)**

RIGHT **A drawing by L.W. Shakespear of the Military Police stockade built at Lung Leh in the Chin Hills in 1889, as a base for three officers and 250 men.**

men also carried a dagger, and some were armed with a 7–8ft (2.1–2.4m) thrusting spear. Abor shields were usually made of interwoven strips of bamboo and were never decorated in any way. They were about 3ft (91cm) long, 20in (50cm) wide and very slightly curved.

B3. ABOR CHIEFTAIN
Chieftains and wealthy warriors wore short-sleeved woollen coats imported from Tibet. These were either sprinkled with small decorative designs, striped, coloured or left plain white (or off-white). Clans appear to have worn their own distinctive patterns – the southern Minyongs and Pasis, for instance, wore 'bluish' coats decorated with white, blue and red designs, other Minyongs wore reddish-brown coats decorated with thin blue or yellow stripes and so on. Their helmets were ornately decorated using materials such as hornbill and crow feathers, boar's tusks, hornbill beaks and pieces of bear, bison or deer-skin dyed red or black. The boar's tusks were normally attached at the front as an additional defence against sword-cuts, the hornbill beak surmounted the crown, and a red-dyed yak tail hung at the back.

The Abors possessed very few firearms, even at the end of the period covered here. However, a few antiquated Tower muskets could be found in the villages nearest to the British frontier, and small numbers of Tibetan matchlocks filtered into more northern districts.

C1. KHAMTI WARRIOR
Khamti costume was very similar to that of the Burmese, consisting of a sheet of chequered cotton cloth folded round the waist and 'looped up' between the legs, a close-fitting cotton or silk jacket, usually dyed blue, and a white turban wrapped round the top-knot into which their long hair was tied. They were typically armed with a *dao* and shield, and some also carried a Chinese matchlock or an antiquated English flintlock that might date back to at least 1780. Their shields were of gilded and lacquered buffalo and rhinoceros hide.

C2. GARO WARRIOR
The Garos wore their hair in a mixture of styles. Some cropped it close, but the majority seem to have worn it medium length and kept off the face with a bead-decorated headband which pushed the hair up brush-like all round the head. Chieftains often wore a loosely tied silk turban instead. A particularly distinctive feature of a Garo's appearance was the collection of up to a dozen or more large brass earrings ('brass curtain rings', as one observer described them), the weight of which stretched their ear-lobes almost as far as the shoulder.

Typical Garo arms were a spear, sword and shield. The characteristic Garo sword was the distinctively shaped *mil'am*; usually about 3ft (91cm) long with a straight, two-edged blade about 2in (5cm) wide, narrowing towards the hilt. Blade and grip were made from a single piece of iron, and the pommel had a sharpened edge enabling it to be stuck in the ground when a warrior halted to rest. (Garo swords were always carried in the hand, and never sheathed in any way.) Bows were not popular. Bamboo crossbows were occasionally seen, but very few firearms.

Shields were about 3ft (91cm) long, 18in (45cm) wide and

ABOVE **A typical group of Sylu Lushais, photographed in the 1880s. Smoking became immensely popular among all the hill-tribes in the course of the 19th century, and most contemporary pictures of Lushais show them sucking on long-stemmed pipes.**

RIGHT **A page from the *Illustrated London News* of 13 April 1889 depicting scenes sketched during the expedition against the Lushais. At the bottom right is Demagiri, a typical frontier outpost of the period.**

roughly rectangular. Three varieties were used, one of bamboo strips, another of 'flat lengths of wood bound together and covered with very thin strips of cane or bamboo' and a third of hide stretched over a wooden frame.

C3. KHASIA WARRIOR
The most distinctive item of Khasia dress comprised a sleeveless, loose-fitting, fringed shirt made of thick hemp, cotton cloth or occasionally eria silk. Though this looked like a jacket done up at the front, it actually consisted of two pieces 'sewn together like a bag, apertures being left for the head and arms'. These shirts were customarily striped, either red and blue or red and white. Another characteristic item of Khasia dress was the *ka tupia shkor*, or 'ear cap', which came down over the ears and had a peak at the front: it was most often red or black.

Khasias were customarily armed with a sword, bow and circular shield. The sword was a sort of double-hander, with

43

a hilt that was up to 60 per cent as long as the blade. Khasia longbows were of bamboo, with a strand of bamboo fibre for a bowstring. In length they varied between 5ft 2in (1.57m) and the height of a man. A few men might also carry spears, and a handful had firearms.

D1. DAFLA WARRIOR

Dafla head-dress typically consisted of a small woven cane cap which had a peak at the back, a serow (deer) horn curving across the crown and a small plume of magpie, pheasant or hornbill feathers. They wore a short, sleeveless shirt of coarse cotton cloth, sometimes striped in blue and red but more often left its natural colour (most often described as 'dirty' or 'sooty' grey). Dozens of cane rings were worn loosely round the lower abdomen, supposedly as a form of body-armour. The hairy-looking rain-cloak, invariably black, was made of bearskin or, more often, plant fibre which closely resembled bearskin. A basketwork haversack worn underneath it carried the warrior's provisions, pipe and tobacco. Supplies of rice and water were also carried in short lengths of bamboo tied together in threes and slung over the shoulder.

Armament comprised a bow, poisoned arrows, a long, straight Tibetan sword, a dagger, and occasionally a rectangular leather shield and a long bamboo spear.

The Eastern Daflas tattooed their faces with a transverse band across the cheeks, while the Apa Tanangs had a T-shaped tattoo below the mouth which reached the point of the chin. The only other important respects in which Apa Tanangs differed from their Dafla cousins were the way in which their hair was more intricately plaited and tightly knotted and the fact that they had a red 'tail' – consisting of strands of spliced cane – hanging down from their belts at the back, almost as far as the knee.

D2. SINGPHO WARRIOR

Singpho dress usually comprised a short, dark blue or black cotton jacket and a chequered cloth 'kilt'. The cotton or silk headscarf was most often white, but it could also be blue, red or chequered. They frequently wore a broad bamboo 'coolie-hat' over this.

This warrior is armed with the traditional Singpho combination of crossbow and *dao*, the latter carried in a distinctive sheath worn across the chest and under the left arm. Its curved blade was 18–24in (45–60cm) long, and 1½in (38mm) wide at the hilt, increasing to 2½in (63mm) at its squared tip. The crossbow was made of hardened bamboo, with a wooden stock, and it fired bamboo bolts which had either fire-hardened points or, less commonly, iron tips. Many substituted a long-barrelled Chinese matchlock, and by about the 1860s some had Tower muskets of *c*.1800 vintage, converted Enfields and even Winchester carbines, all obtained in China's Yunnan province. Rectangular buffalo-hide shields, 4ft (1.2m) long, and hide or bamboo helmets were also sometimes encountered in the early part of this period.

D3. MISHMI *GAM*

Mishmi chiefs, or *gams*, wore Tibetan woollen coats, generally dyed deep red, sometimes 'ornamented with white spots, which are preserved from the action of the dye by tying'. Bow and *dao* were characteristic arms, though chiefs

A drawing depicting (left to right) a Lushai, a Poi, another Lushai and a Sokté. Pois differed from Lushais in tying their hair above the forehead, while the Soktés wore theirs short and 'standing out like the tresses of Medusa'. (R.G. Woodthorpe, *The Lushai Expedition*, 1873)

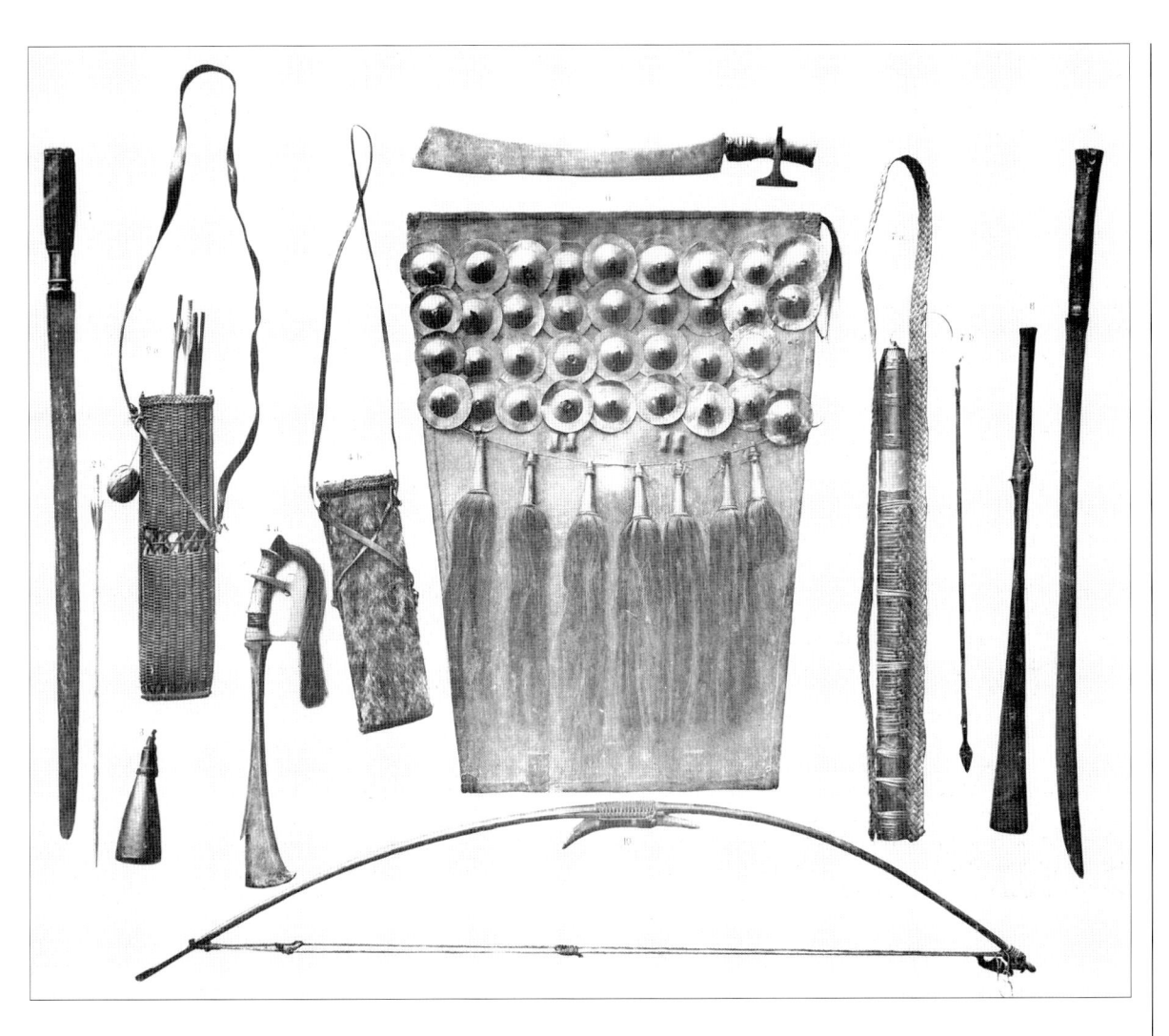

frequently substituted a straight Tibetan sword for the latter. Their arrows were poisoned with aconite. Sources of the first half of the 19th century indicate that an 8ft (2.4m) thrusting spear was then considered more important than the bow. Crossbows were also used, and on occasion Tibetan matchlocks are mentioned as being carried by chiefs. Shields, where carried, were oblong and made of buffalo hide.

Ordinary Mishmi dress consisted of a brief, dark blue loincloth with a red or yellow stripe running though it and a sleeveless, sack-like jacket made of blue and red (or brown) striped woollen cloth, worn open at the front. Head-dress comprised either a large fur cap or a wicker helmet. Most Mishmis wore their hair long and tied in a top-knot, but the Chulikata, or 'crop-haired Mishmis', earned their name by cropping their hair round the sides of the head 'so as to give them the appearance of wearing a mushroom-shaped hat'.

E1. KUKI WARRIOR

Up until about the 1860s the majority of Kukis wore, at most, a loincloth, a white or dark blue cotton sheet wrapped round the body (like that of figure E2) and a *pagri*. Their hair was worn long and tied in an untidy knot at the back of the head.

Weapons of Chittagong frontier hill-tribes, including a Lushai quiver (left) and powder flask, Shendu swords (top and lower left), quiver (right) and shield, and a Lushai pellet-bow. (Emil Riebeck, *The Chittagong Hill-Tribes*, 1885)

Note the circular tattoo, which frequently appeared on the outside of one or both forearms.

At the beginning of the Victorian period most Kukis were armed with a bow, *dao* and shield, and sometimes a spear, but by the second half of the 19th century many carried a musket in place of the bow. The *dao* had a brass or wooden handle, the latter type being either covered in leather or bound with hair or cane and lacquered, with a tuft of red or white goat's hair attached to the end of the hilt. Bows were made of bamboo. The arrows were kept in a quiver made of a section of bamboo about 22in (56cm) long, with a lid. For protection this warrior carries a typical trapezoid hide shield and wears a corselet made of buffalo or rhinoceros hide. However, such body armour was probably relatively uncommon.

E2. LUSHAI WARRIOR

Lushai dress comprised a small white loincloth and a cotton sheet about 7ft (2.1m) long and 5ft (1.5m) wide, which came in various colours but was usually white (generally described as 'dirty white' or 'greyish white' but sometimes as 'clean and bright'), most often with a single dark blue stripe or a pair of stripes running through it. The best, however, were dark blue with a crimson or yellow stripe, or 'a species of tartan' which had 'a few stripes of white, yellow or red, or all three interwoven into it'. Many wore these sheets even in combat, sometimes rolling them down round the waist.

Though the Lushai were well equipped with firearms, the majority of these weapons were obsolete flintlock muskets. Some dated back as far as the middle of the 18th century, and the majority seem to have been manufactured in George III's reign. Some were re-stocked locally, aping the shape of the European original but with a thinner butt and a pronounced bend. Stocks and butts were invariably decorated with simple patterns of red, black and, to a lesser extent, yellow lacquer. As well as a firearm and *dao* some men still carried buffalo-hide shields (like that of figure E1).

E3. CHIN WARRIOR

Though some Chins knotted their long hair at the nape of the neck like the Lushais, others wore top-knots tied at the front of the head and wrapped in a headscarf. They customarily wore little clothing beyond a white mantle rolled round the shoulders or tied round the waist, sometimes even going without the loincloth, which was invariably blue. Only the clothes of chiefs were decorated in any way, usually in stripes or tartans. The separate piece of cloth hanging at the back of his legs from bits of string passing diagonally across his chest was intended to give him 'something warm to sit upon when the ground is cold'. He also wears the nearest Chin equivalent to armour, described in a report of 1893 as 'a strip of buffalo hide bent over and about nine inches to one foot broad, reaching from the waist in front to the small of the back behind. It is worn across the left shoulder like the sash of a military officer, the ends being tied together at the right side with a string'.

Though by the 1880s up to 75 per cent of many Chin war-parties were armed with flintlock muskets, often more than a century old, this man still carries the traditional bamboo bow. These were 2½–4ft (0.75–1.2m) long. The barbed, iron-headed bamboo arrows were not poisoned, but were re-used without ever being cleaned, which was almost as bad. Described as being about the thickness of a pencil and, at most, only about 18in (45cm) long, they were fletched with bamboo fibre, leaves or feathers. They were carried in a bamboo quiver at the left side, with a bamboo or lacquered canework lid (attached by a string), sometimes decorated with red beads.

Other popular Chin weapons comprised the *dao*, kept in a sheath worn on the back; the spear, which was usually about 5ft (1.5m) long and very heavy, since as much as half or even two-thirds of its length was iron, with only a short section of wood joining the blade's long socket to an equally long butt-spike; and the dagger, carried in a bone scabbard attached to the right side of the leather breastplate described above. Trapezoid buffalo-hide shields slightly longer than that of figure E1 were still relatively commonplace in the 1870s but were disappearing from use by the 1890s.

F1. KUKI OR LUSHAI CHIEF

Chiefs of the Chin-Lushai peoples dressed very much the same from tribe to tribe. The two characteristic aspects of their dress which distinguished them from ordinary tribesmen

Assault on a Lushai village by men of the Cachar Military Police Battalion in 1889. (*Illustrated London News*, 6 December 1890)

The village of a Tlantlang Chin chief named Hausata comes under fire on 20 March 1889. He had been responsible for wiping out a survey party in Chittagong in February 1888. (*Illustrated London News*, 11 May 1889)

were that their mantles were coloured or patterned, most often in a broad check pattern, and that they wore a large turban decorated with a plume of downy feathers, ribbons of red-dyed goat's hair, and strings of cowrie shells. They were also invariably armed with a musket.

F2. SHENDU WARRIOR
The Shendus knotted their long hair over the forehead, securing it with a brass hairpin. Other than a narrow white loincloth, his only garment is the usual cotton sheet of the Chin-Lushai family. That worn here is the type intended for everyday use, which was plain white. Chieftains, and warriors attending ceremonial functions, substituted dark blue, red or black sheets, decorated with embroidery and one or more white or red stripes. Some were made of cloth imported from Burma and were chequered in blue and white or shades of brown. Many warriors bore one or more simple tattoos on their arms, legs, shoulders and chest – usually a circle, a bison head (on the chest) and devices resembling sequences of the letters X, W or M.

Armament was most commonly a *dao*, a shield and a short spear or (after about 1840) a musket. The *dao* was 18–22in (45–56cm) from its tip to the end of its bamboo handle. It was not usually kept in a sheath, but was simply stuffed into the waistband of the loincloth behind the back or carried in the usual shoulder-bag. What firearms they had consisted of old Tower flintlocks 'marked with dates somewhere round 1815'. These had the same red, black and yellow lacquered stocks as those of the Lushais.

F3. MANIPURI SEPOY
Uniforms were not widespread, and a detachment of Manipuri soldiers seen in 1890 was fairly typical in having only about three completely uniformed men in its ranks. What constituted a 'complete' uniform seems to have comprised only a jacket and belt, with the jacket usually either red or white. The soldier depicted here is based on a photograph of the Manipuri contingent which relieved Kohima in 1879. He is characteristically barefoot.

Britain had supplied the Manipuri army with 750 percussion muskets in 1879 to replace some of its flintlocks, and by 1890 its armament consisted predominantly of Tower muskets and Enfield, Snider and Martini rifles. However, not all Manipuri soldiers had firearms, and many substituted a spear. In addition the majority of regular soldiers carried their own swords (significantly it seems they were not issued with bayonets) and some carried shields for use in close combat.

G1. SYLHET LIGHT INFANTRY, 1837
After wearing a red uniform in 1824–7, by 1835 the Sylhet LI had changed to dark green with black facings, 'bastion loops' and *pagri*. Native shoes were worn. A Kilmarnock cap was substituted for the *pagri* in 1844. Men were armed with the Brown Bess musket until 1872, and a kukri was probably carried from the outset, even though it was not officially authorised until 1881.

G2. 44TH BENGAL NATIVE INFANTRY, 1875
The uniform remained dark green with black facings, though headwear now consisted of a dark green Kilmarnock cap for Gurkhas and other hill-peoples, with a 'round black ball or tuft' on the crown (or a red toorie or tassel, in the case of the 42nd) and a silver unit badge on the front. After 1866 Punjabi soldiers of Assam regiments substituted a black *pagri*.

Though this photograph was taken early in the 20th century, the costume of these Abor chiefs is identical to that of their 19th-century counterparts.

Trousers were of the baggy 'zouave' variety, worn with black puttees and black boots. Equipment was black leather. The Enfield had replaced the Brown Bess in 1872, and the Snider was introduced in 1874.

G3. SEMA NAGA IN BRITISH SERVICE
Nagas participated in several British expeditions, technically in the role of coolies, though they took their weapons with them in the hope of taking a few heads. The Sema wore their hair very short except for a basin-shaped patch on the crown, and they tattooed their faces. Those in British service were distinguished only by a rag with a unit number painted on it tied round their head. Typically they were armed with a spear, *dao* and shield. The shield was about 4ft (1.2m) long, made of interwoven bamboo matting bound with cane. The *dao* was sheathed behind the back in a wooden block 8in (20cm) long by 2½in (6.3cm) wide, 'pierced from top to bottom by a slit about six inches long and broad enough to admit the blade, but too narrow to let the handle slip through'.

H1. FRONTIER POLICE c.1848–68
It was only from about 1848 that the Levy or Militia units from which the Frontier Police evolved were first issued with a uniform. It consisted of 'black' (doubtless, in reality, very dark rifle-green) jacket and trousers, black Kilmarnock cap and black leather waist-belt and crossbelts. Native shoes were worn (if any were worn at all). No haversack was provided, however, and it was customary for police units to carry their spare kit and provisions rolled in a sheet tied round the torso. As late as the 1880s an officer observed of the typical Frontier Policeman: 'On his back he carried all his belongings and food for several days, wrapped in a large cloth the ends of which were tied across his chest and which served him as a blanket at night. Hanging round him by strings would be his *ghi chunga* and an odd parcel or two, and, as likely as not, he would carry an aged, corpulent gamp as well as his rifle.' He was armed with a Brown Bess musket and bayonet, and a short sword, which was replaced by a kukri in the 1860s. At this date the majority of Frontier Police constables were Cacharis, Gurkhas and Shans. The Cacharis among them often wore a black *pagri* in place of the Kilmarnock cap.

H2. FRONTIER POLICE 1868–85
From 1868 most units on the North-East Frontier wore dark blue uniforms with white metal buttons and white piping round the cuffs and collar and down the trouser seam. The Chittagong Frontier Police, however, continued to wear rifle-green until 1891. Officially the dark blue Kilmarnock cap then worn was supposed to have had a silver bugle badge on the front, but the photograph from which this figure comes shows a badge with the letters 'FP' instead. Equipment was still of black leather. Black puttees or stiff brown canvas gaiters were also issued, plus European-style black boots. However, the latter seem to have been worn rarely on campaign. 'After his first march his boots were generally carried on his pack,' wrote a British officer in 1884, 'being slung round his neck by the laces.' The Enfield rifle replaced the Brown Bess at some point during this period, probably around 1871, and this was replaced in turn by the Snider in 1881. The short sword previously carried was replaced by a kukri by (or in) 1868: it was usually carried at the back of the belt.

H3. MILITARY POLICE 1885–1901
The Military Police battalions into which the Frontier Police battalions had been reorganised in 1882–3 at first continued to wear the uniform of figure H2: it survived in use in some areas until around 1887, even though khaki uniforms were introduced in 1885. The bugle cap-badge was changed to two crossed kukris in 1885, even though the source for this figure still shows a bugle cap-badge being worn. In 1887 narrow scarlet piping was added to the collar, cuffs and trouser seams. Equipment was brown leather. Though bandoliers were used for some years, they were eventually abandoned as impractical for use in the jungle, where they constantly snagged on branches. The Snider rifle remained in use until as late as 1901, when it was finally replaced by the Martini-Henry.